SCHOLASTIC
LITERATURE GUIDE

Harry Potter
and the Sorcerer's Stone

by
J. K. Rowling

Written by Linda Ward Beech
Cover design by Vincent Ceci and Jaime Lucero
Interior design by Grafica, Inc.
Original cover and interior design by Drew Hires
Interior illustrations by Mona Mark

Jacket cover from HARRY POTTER AND THE SORCERER'S STONE by J. K. Rowling.
Published by Arthur A. Levine Books, an imprint of Scholastic Press.
Jacket art © 1998 by Mary GrandPré. Jacket design by Mary GrandPré and David Saylor.

ISBN 0-439-21116-6
Copyright © 2000 by Scholastic Inc.
Printed in the U.S.A.

Table of Contents

BEFORE READING THE BOOK

EXPLORING THE BOOK

Chapters 1–6

Chapters 7–12

Chapters 13–17

SUMMARIZING THE BOOK

STUDENT REPRODUCIBLES

Before Reading the Book

SUMMARY

Harry Potter lives in the cupboard under the stairs at his relatives' home until he receives letters inviting him to the Hogwarts School of Witchcraft and Wizardry. Harry, an orphan, learns that his parents were well-known wizards who did not die in a car crash but were killed by Voldemort, the Lord of Darkness. Harry also finds that he is famous in the wizard world because he survived Voldemort's attack. Against his uncle's wishes, Harry leaves for the school where his adventures begin. He makes new friends, becomes a member of Gryffindor house, and earns the role of Seeker on his house's Quidditch team. As Harry and his friends study the world of spells and potions, they also uncover a mystery: A three-headed dog guards a trapdoor at the school. Bravery, curiosity, and magic help the students confront the evil of Voldemort and win the house cup for Gryffindor.

Harry Potter
The Cupboard under the Stairs
4 Privet Drive
Little Whinging
Surrey

CHARACTERS

People

Harry Potter	main character
Lily and James Potter	Harry's parents
Vernon and Petunia Dursley	Harry's uncle and aunt
Dudley Dursley	Harry's cousin
Albus Dumbledore	headmaster of Hogwarts
Professor Minerva McGonagall	Transfiguration teacher
Voldemort	Lord of Darkness and Evil
Madam Pomfrey	school nurse
Rubeus Hagrid	Hogwarts groundskeeper
Mrs. Figg	Dursley neighbor
Madame Pince	Hogwarts librarian
Piers Polkiss	Dudley's friend
Professor Quirrell	Defense of Dark Arts teacher
Griphook	Gringotts goblin
Madame Malkin	seller of robes
Mr. Ollivander	seller of wands
Ron Weasley	Harry's friend
Mrs. Weasley	Ron's mother
Percy, Fred, George, Bill, Charlie, and Ginny	Ron's brothers and sister
Neville Longbottom	Harry's friend
Hermione Granger	Harry's friend
Draco Malfoy	Hogwarts bully
Crabbe and Goyle	Malfoy's friends
Professor Severus Snape	Potions teacher
Professor Binns	History of Magic teacher
Professor Sprout	Herbology teacher
Madame Hooch	Flying teacher
Mr. Argus Filch	Hogwarts caretaker
Oliver Wood	Gryffindor Quidditch captain
Nicholas Flamel	maker of Sorcerer's Stone

Ghosts

Peeves, Fat Friar, Nearly Headless Nick, Bloody Baron

Animals

Hedwig	Harry's owl
Scabbers	Ron's rat
Trevor	Neville's toad
Mrs. Norris	Filch's cat
Fang	Hagrid's dog
Fluffy	three-headed dog
Norbert	Hagrid's dragon
Ronan, Bane, Firenze	centaurs

ABOUT THE AUTHOR

For J. K. Rowling, writing is her greatest pleasure. She wrote her first book (still unpublished) at the age of six. Says Rowling, "I have always written, and I know that I always will; I would be writing even if I hadn't been published." J. K. Rowling got the idea for the Harry Potter books while on a train from Manchester to London. When she began writing the first Harry Potter book in a café in Edinburgh, Scotland, Rowling was on welfare with an infant daughter. Helped by a grant from the Scottish Arts Council, Rowling took five years to finish *Harry Potter and the Sorcerer's Stone*. During that time she was also planning the six sequels, one for each of Harry's years at Hogwarts. Says Rowling, "It was my life's ambition to see a book I had written on a shelf in a bookshop."

Rowling is a graduate of Exeter University and a former teacher. In addition to the British Isles, she has also lived in Portugal. Her favorite holiday is Halloween, when she holds a big party for her friends and their children.

LITERATURE CONNECTIONS

Other books by J. K. Rowling:
• *Harry Potter and the Chamber of Secrets*
• *Harry Potter and the Prisoner of Azkaban*

VOCABULARY

The words on the following list may be unfamiliar to students. Have students work in groups of three or four. Give each group a copy of the list. Point out that students will need to use a dictionary for this activity. Then challenge the groups to put as many of the words as they can into four or five different categories. They can use categories you provide or ones that they make up. Tell students to be prepared to defend their word choices for each category. For example:

Geology	Botany	Unusual Things	Ways of Moving
specimen	asphodel	treacle	rummaging
amber	aconite	tripe	swaggered

beefy	tawny	tantrum	rummaging	specimen
gibber	knickerbockers	amber	gargoyle	ruefully
cinema	apothecary	swarthy	hurtled	stalagmite
stalactite	ravine	miniscule	emporium	yew
prefect	alchemy	sidled	tripe	tinge
riffraff	lurched	swaggered	treacle	subtle
cauldron	ensnaring	asphodel	bezoar	aconite
nettles	flitted	taunting	luminous	biased
petrified	hygienic	confiscated	abysmal	warlock
fungi	burly	berserk		

THINKING ABOUT THEMES

Before beginning the book, talk about the concept of themes with students. Remind students that a theme is the central idea or message that an author conveys in a book. Explain that usually the theme is communicated through the characters, plot, and setting. As students read *Harry Potter and the Sorcerer's Stone*, have them look for examples of the theme of good prevailing over evil. Suggest that students note other themes as well—loyalty, bravery, truth, and the power of love.

THINKING ABOUT GENRE

You may wish to point out that *Harry Potter* is a fantasy—a book that depends largely on imaginative possibilities not found in real life. Although the story begins in the real world, it soon moves into the magical world of Hogwarts with its potions, spells, and suspension of the laws of nature, time, and place. Mention that other books that follow this pattern include *A Wrinkle in Time, Peter Pan,* and *The Lion, the Witch and the Wardrobe.*

GETTING STARTED

Try the following strategies as you introduce the book to the class:

- Write the book title on the chalkboard, and ask students if they know what a sorcerer is. Discuss the word and, if necessary, have students look up its definition.
- Draw students' attention to the book cover. What does the illustration show? What is the boy doing? How would students describe the boy? What mood does the illustration convey?
- Ask students to look closely at the type used for Harry's name in the book title. What relationship can they see between Harry and the letter *p* in *Potter*? Encourage students to speculate about what this might mean.
- Invite students to read through the chapter titles in the table of contents. Suggest that they write down a prediction about each chapter based on its title. Have students save their predictions to reread after they finish a chapter.

Exploring the Book

WHAT HAPPENS

Harry Potter arrives at the Dursleys under very pec
liar circumstances. Although his aunt and uncle
aren't at all happy at having Harry live with them,
people all over the country are rejoicing at the
"boy who lived." Ten difficult years later, Harry
begins to get mysterious letters. Despite Uncle
Vernon's efforts to keep the letters from him, Harry
finally learns that he has been invited to attend
the Hogwarts School of Witchcraft and Wizardry.
He also learns that his parents were renowned

wizards who were killed by the evil Voldemort. Accompanied by Hagrid, Harry shops
for his schoolbooks and materials, including wizard robes, a wand, and an owl.
When Harry finally leaves for school, he meets other new students, including Ron,
Hermione, and Neville, on the train.

QUESTIONS TO TALK ABOUT
COMPREHENSION AND RECALL

1. What signs foretell of Harry's arrival at the Dursleys when he's a little boy? (*owls fluttering by in daylight; cat reading map; strangely dressed people acting excited; overheard conversations about Harry; downpour of shooting stars*)

2. Why do his aunt and uncle treat Harry so badly? (*They don't approve of wizards; they think they're abnormal. They favor their own son.*)

3. What are some of the inexplicable things that happen to Harry at the Dursleys? (*His hair grows back the next day after Aunt Petunia cuts it; he is found on the roof of the school when Dudley's gang chases him; he has strange dreams; he frees the snake at the zoo.*)

4. Why does Uncle Vernon take the family to a shack on a rock in the sea? (*He doesn't want Harry's letters to reach them.*)

5. Why does Hagrid get so mad at the Dursleys? (*They haven't given Harry his letters or told him about Hogwarts and his parents.*)

6. How did Harry get a scar on his forehead? (*Voldemort's evil curse touched him there.*)

HIGHER-LEVEL THINKING SKILLS

7. How does Harry feel about Dudley? (*He doesn't like him; Dudley's a bully and very selfish, lazy, and spoiled.*)

8. Why does Uncle Vernon tell Harry he can leave the cupboard under the stairs and sleep in a bedroom? (*He is upset by Harry's letter, which is addressed to him in the cupboard.*)

9. Why don't people want to say Voldemort's name? (*He is so evil; the name recalls dark powers and bad events.*)

10. How does Hagrid feel about Albus Dumbledore? (*He admires him greatly; is very protective of him.*)

11. Why does Harry trust Hagrid even though Hagrid tells him unbelievable things? (*Possible: Hagrid is kind to him.*)

12. Why does Harry find Ron so intriguing? (*He comes from a family of wizards and is familiar with magic.*)

LITERARY ELEMENTS

13. Character: What similarities does the author show between Malfoy and Dudley? (*Both are arrogant and can intimidate their parents; both are bullies.*)

PERSONAL RESPONSE

14. How would you feel if you discovered you were a wizard?

15. What do the names of the four Hogwarts houses—Ravenclaw, Hufflepuff, Slytherin, and Gryffindor—suggest to you? Which one would you want to be in? Why?

CROSS-CURRICULAR ACTIVITIES

ART: *What a Scene*
Invite students to illustrate a favorite scene from the story so far. Students might work in pastels or tempera paint. Encourage students to refer to the text for details of the characters and settings they choose to portray. Have students share their finished illustrations with the class and ask the class to identify the scene.

MUSIC: *Sound Effects*
Suggest that students select appropriate music to enhance a scene in the book. For example, they might choose music for an angry scene, a funny scene, or a scary one. Have students explain why they chose the music they did, and, if possible, have them play a tape of the music while they read aloud the scene.

LANGUAGE ARTS: *Words for Wizards*
Point out that part of the fun of the book is that the author uses such clever and funny names. Give the following examples: Leaky Cauldron, Griphook, Flourish and Blotts, Muggles. Ask students what each of these names suggests to them. Why? Talk about why the author might use such names. Then share with the class that the author makes up many names and also collects unusual names. In an interview, she pointed out that Hedwig is the name of a saint and Dumbledore is an Old English word that means "bumblebee."

TEACHER TIP

Ask students to look on page 66 at the list of books Harry needs for school. What examples of wordplay can they find?

WHAT HAPPENS

At school, Harry meets his new professors, fellow students, and the resident ghosts. He is relieved to be chosen by the sorting hat for Gryffindor, along with Ron and Hermione. At the opening banquet, Dumbledore warns students to stay away from a corridor on the third floor. Harry is disconcerted that so many students seem to know who he is, and he gets the distinct impression that Professor Snape doesn't like him. While rescuing Neville's Remembrall from the bully Malfoy, Harry demonstrates his broomstick skills. As a result, he becomes the Seeker on the Gryffindor Quidditch team and even gets a Nimbus Two Thousand broom. One night he, Ron, Neville, and Hermione accidentally discover a three-headed dog guarding a trapdoor in the forbidden corridor. Harry is sure

the dog is guarding something that Hagrid took from the bank at Gringotts. At Christmas, Harry gets an invisibility cloak from an unknown giver. While trying it out, he discovers the Mirror of Erised and sees his family in it.

QUESTIONS TO TALK ABOUT

COMPREHENSION AND RECALL

1. Why is Harry so fearful of being in Slytherin? (*He knows it's associated with Voldemort.*)

2. Why don't Harry and Ron go with Percy to the dorms when the troll is in the dungeon? (*Harry realizes that Hermione doesn't know about the troll; they have to tell her.*)

3. Why does Hermione lie about the troll to Professor McGonagall? (*She lies to keep Harry and Ron from getting into trouble.*)

HIGHER-LEVEL THINKING SKILLS

4. What does Harry's nervousness about the sorting hat tell you about him? (*He's afraid there will be a test and he will fail; he doesn't like to fail. He's competitive. He doesn't want to be a Slytherin.*)

5. How does Harry feel about his fame? (*He'd prefer to be just one of the students.*)

6. Why does Harry get on his broomstick when Madame Hooch tells the class not to? (*He can't stand to see Malfoy take advantage of Neville by hiding the Remembrall.*)

7. How would you describe the way Lee Jordan reports the Quidditch match? (*He's angry about fouls and shows it. He's on the side of Gryffindor; he's not impartial.*)

8. Why can the mirror be dangerous? (*A viewer dwells on dreams and forgets to live in the present.*)

LITERARY ELEMENTS

9. Plot: How does Malfoy help Harry get on the Quidditch team? (*He teases Harry about the Remembrall and when Harry goes after it, Professor McGonagall sees how good he is.*) Is Harry above the rules, just lucky, or is the author simply trying to advance the plot? (*Answers will vary.*)

PERSONAL RESPONSE

10. Hogwarts is all new to Harry. How do you feel in new situations?

11. Is Harry right to let Malfoy bully him into a duel? Why or why not?

12. What would you see in the Mirror of Erised?

TEACHER TIP

Be sure students translate the mirror's inscription on page 207. ("I show not your face but your heart's desire.") Discuss why Dumbledore says the mirror gives "neither knowledge nor truth."

CROSS-CURRICULAR ACTIVITIES

WRITING: *Magic for Me*

Harry Potter has several magic objects—a wand, his Nimbus Two Thousand broomstick, and his invisibility cloak. Have students choose one item and write a story about an adventure they might have with it. Encourage students to illustrate their adventure tales and share them with the class.

TEACHER TIP

Pass on the following to students: When asked what advice she would give to young writers, J. K. Rowling had this word: "Persevere!"

ART: *Getting Around Hogwarts*

Remind students that the author describes many different parts of Hogwarts, from the banquet hall to the classrooms, corridors, and dormitories. Challenge students to work with partners to make floor plans of the school based on the descriptions in the book. Post these plans in the room and use them to identify where various episodes of the story take place.

DRAMA: *Quidditch Broadcast*

Students might do a play-by-play radio broadcast of the Quidditch match between Slytherin and Gryffindor. Students can use the dialogue in the book or invent their own. Suggest that students include commercial breaks for products that wizard consumers might use.

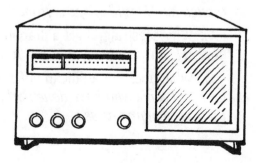

WHAT HAPPENS

Harry discovers who Nicholas Flamel is and figures out that the three-headed dog must be guarding the Sorcerer's Stone. Hagrid breeds a dragon in his hut, which Harry and his friends help send off to Ron's brother in Romania. To serve a detention, Harry, Malfoy, Hermione, and Neville help Hagrid look for an injured unicorn in the Forbidden Forest. When Harry finds it, a cloaked figure is drinking its blood. Harry is saved by a centaur named Firenze who tells him the figure is Voldemort trying to stay alive until he can get the Elixir of Life from the Sorcerer's Stone. Harry realizes that Voldemort is close to reaching the stone despite all the charms keeping it safe. He also thinks Snape is helping Voldemort. Harry, Ron, and Hermione get past the three-headed dog and through the trapdoor. Harry passes through a wall of fire to find not Snape but Quirrell, inhabited by Voldemort, attempting to get the Stone. They struggle; Dumbledore arrives just in time, and the Stone and Harry are saved.

QUESTIONS TO TALK ABOUT

COMPREHENSION AND RECALL

1. How is Harry's kindness to Neville repaid? (*Neville gives Harry a card from a Chocolate Frog; the card tells who Flamel is.*)

2. How does Norbert get Harry and his friends in trouble? (*They are caught coming down from the tower after sending Norbert to Romania.*)

3. Why does Voldemort drink unicorn blood? (*He drinks it to stay alive until he can get to the Sorcerer's Stone.*)

4. Why can't Quirrell touch Harry? (*Harry is protected by the power of his mother's love.*)

5. Why does Neville get ten points? (*He gets them because of his bravery in standing up to his friends.*)

HIGHER-LEVEL THINKING SKILLS

6. How does Harry show his loyalty to the Quidditch team? (*He plays even though he's fearful of spells from Snape.*)

7. Why does Hagrid get a dragon even though it's against the law and dangerous? (*He loves animals and has always wanted a dragon.*)

8. What does Ronan mean when he says, "Always the innocent are the first victims"? (*People who have done nothing wrong get hurt when other people fight for their particular causes.*)

9. Why does Firenze save Harry even though Bane is against it? (*He knows Harry will aid in fighting the evil of Voldemort.*)

10. How do the talents of each student—Harry, Hermione, and Ron—come in handy when each approaches the Stone? (*Hermione uses spells and logic she has learned; Harry uses his Seeker skills; Ron is a good chess player.*)

11. Dumbledore says that the truth "is a beautiful and terrible thing, and should therefore be treated with great caution." What does he mean by this? (*Possible: The truth can be hurtful as well as helpful. You should think before using it.*)

LITERARY ELEMENTS

12. Foreshadowing: How is the role of the Mirror of Erised in saving the Stone foreshadowed? (*Harry has used the mirror before and learned about its powers; he knows it will only show what the viewer desires.*)

PERSONAL RESPONSE

13. What would you do with a Sorcerer's Stone? Why?

14. How would you treat a student like Malfoy?

CROSS-CURRICULAR ACTIVITIES

LITERATURE: *The Sorcerer's Stone*

Review with students that the Sorcerer's Stone is "a legendary substance with astonishing powers" and can produce the Elixir of Life, which makes a drinker immortal. Ask students to find and report on other literary examples of this theme of immortality. One example they might look at is *Tuck Everlasting* by Natalie Babbitt.

LOGIC: *Chasing Chessmen*

Recall with students that Ron is a good chess player and uses his skills to get him, Harry, and Hermione across a room in their search for the Stone. Invite students who play chess to bring in sets and teach a partner who doesn't know the game.

WRITING: *Mystical, Magical Creatures*

This book is populated by many imaginary creatures, including unicorns, a phoenix, a dragon, centaurs, gargoyles, gorgons, trolls, griffins, and vampires. Have students choose one creature to research. Then ask students to write a description telling about its history, powers, and function in literature and art. Instruct students to include an illustration of their creature as well.

Summarizing the Book

PUTTING IT ALL TOGETHER

Choose from among the following activities to help students summarize and appreciate *Harry Potter and the Sorcerer's Stone*.

CLASS PROJECT: *Prizes and Praise*

Tell students that *Harry Potter and the Sorcerer's Stone* won the 1997 National Book Award in the United Kingdom and the 1997 Gold Medal Smarties Prize. It was also shortlisted for the Carnegie Medal, the British equivalent of the Newbery Medal. In the United States the book was an ALA Notable Book, the New York Public Library Best Book of the Year 1998, and *Parenting* Book of the Year 1998. *Harry Potter and the Sorcerer's Stone* has been a bestseller in the United States and in many other countries. Have the class brainstorm a list of at least ten reasons that this book is such a success. Encourage students to explain the reasons they suggest.

GROUP PROJECT: *Harry Potter Glossary*

Students might work in groups to compile made-up, eccentric, and unusual words from the book into a glossary. Students should begin by listing all the possible words they might include. They should define each word from its context in the story. In some cases students might want to illustrate words. Suggest that students use a separate page for each letter of the alphabet and plan to add more words as they read other Harry Potter books.

PARTNER PROJECT: *Tell It Again*

Have students work with partners for this activity. Review that the author tells the story as it happens to Harry. Ask students to retell scenes from the book to each other from the point of view of another character. For example, they might tell about hunting for the unicorn in the forest from the point of view of Hagrid or Malfoy.

INDIVIDUAL PROJECT: *Comic Book Scenes*

Artistically inclined students might retell a scene from the book in comic book form. Encourage students to use dialogue from the story in their speech balloons.

Not Slytherin, eh?
Are you sure?

EVALUATION IDEAS

Ask students to come up with a set of rubrics to use in assessing one of the summarizing projects. For example, a rubric for the glossary might include these objectives:
• Did students include all the relevant words in the glossary?
• Did students do a thorough and accurate job of defining the words?
• Did students organize the glossary well?
• Did students show care in their execution and presentation of the assignment?

Answers for Reproducibles

page 14: Textbook titles at Hogwarts—*The Standard Book of Spells, A History of Magic, Magical Theory, A Beginner's Guide to Transfiguration, One Thousand Magical Herbs and Fungi, Magical Drafts and Potions, Fantastic Beasts and Where to Find Them, The Dark Forces: A Guide to Self-Protection*; Subjects at Hogwarts— Defense of Dark Arts, Transfiguration, Herbology, History of Magic, Charms, Potions; Sports at Hogwarts—Quidditch; Special Events at Hogwarts—start-of-term banquet with Sorting Ceremony, Halloween feast, Christmas dinner, end-of-the-year feast. Students' answers will vary for their own school.

page 15: 1. It is used to guard the Sorcerer's Stone. It shows the viewer what he or she most desires. 2. It sorts students into houses at Hogwarts. 3. Players ride them in the air in the game of Quidditch. 4. Owls are used to deliver the mail.
5. Portraits serve as the entrances to the dormitories.

page 16: 1. factual 2. fanciful 3. factual 4. fanciful 5. fanciful 6. factual 7. fanciful 8. fanciful 9. fanciful 10. factual

Name: _____

Two Schools of Thought

The Hogwarts School for Witchcraft and Wizardry differs from your school in numerous ways.
Fill in the chart to compare the two schools.

Hogwarts

My School

	Hogwarts	My School
Textbook Titles		
Subjects		
Sports		
Special Events		

Scholastic Literature Guide • Harry Potter and the Sorcerer's Stone

Name: _____

Unusual Uses

At Hogwarts, some everyday things have special uses. Tell how each of these is used at the school.

1.

_____
_____
_____

2.

_____
_____
_____

3.

_____
_____
_____

4.

_____
_____
_____

5.

_____
_____
_____

Name: _____

Factual or Fanciful

Some of the things that happen in *Harry Potter and the Sorcerer's Stone* are factual—they could actually happen. Others are fanciful or imaginary. Write "factual" or "fanciful" next to each statement below.

1. Harry lives with an aunt, uncle, and cousin. _____

2. Harry attends a school for wizards. _____

3. Some of the students are bullies. _____

4. Goblins work in the bank. _____

5. People in photographs can move. _____

6. The students sleep in dormitories. _____

7. A three-headed dog guards a trapdoor. _____

8. Hagrid obtains a dragon's egg. _____

9. Harry is rescued by a centaur. _____

10. The students take exams at the end of the term. _____